MARCH TWENTY-FIFTH

JEREME WESLEY

QUOTE

March 25th

"The effectual fervent prayer of a righteous man availeth much" – *James 5:16*

DEDICATION

"This book is written in loving memory of a young lady whom I had and still have the pleasure of calling my sister-love. Kia Dawn V. Sparks left to be with the Lord and her loving father in the year 2012. She was headed to nursing school with prayers, paper, pen, and a dream. With faith in God she knew that she could do all things through Christ who strengthened her (Philippians 4:13). This book is also relaying the same message Kia carried that no matter how big your storm may be, God has the ultimate power, last say so, and he will bring you out." —Jereme Reshon

Special Thanks to my parents, who never said, "I told you so." To the woman who was willing to care for my children as her own had I went home to be with God. To the woman who had no problem being there every step of the way on my way to recovery and still today is my Hero! Dora Ann Wesley, I love you, Mommy. Daddy, your work has never gone unnoticed, especially in the eyes of your daughter. You've shown me to work through any and every obstacle. I love you, Daddy!"

BLURB

Having guidance from both parents who were strong in their walks with God, Jereme was knowledgeable of her calling and position in life at an early age but decided to take an alternative route. It pin-points one traumatic event that occurs in her life, that later on built a solid foundation for her to reclaim and gain back everything she lost in the midst of her trials and tribulations, while all along walking in her purpose.

This is an encouragement to *you* that the storms sent your way aren't meant to blow you, but to grow you! God wants to refine you into the person he has called you to be so that you may live life full of prosperity! You are more than a conqueror! Blessings!

INTRODUCTION

"Ever wondered what a modern-day miracle would be like? We know what God can do for the sick, and we know what he did for the blind man, but has a prayer for healing and restoration from the righteous ever been manifested right before your eyes for someone you know or maybe even you? Well, it has for me.

Take a ride with me down memory lane as I share my testimony of how God stepped in and performed a task that was deemed as impossible to men, which gave me life so I could live again! Things may seem out of your control. You may have even stepped out of His will, but the good news is He hasn't forgotten about you. It's not too late to come back. If He did it for me, He can do it for you!

-Jereme Reshon

CHAPTER ONE

As a nineteen-year-old, I felt like I was grown, or at a stage in my life where I could make decisions for myself and they would just about be the right decisions for me. Well, that's how society puts it, when you have a baby, or in my case babies, at an early age, right? I finished high school by the grace of God and was working and in college to become a medical assistant. To top it off, at the time, I had the finest guy in my life. Everything about him was wrong, but it seemed so right! After going through a lot with him, I knew it was time to move in together, not expecting to be faced with some of the biggest obstacles that I would later overcome.

"Baby? Baby, you up?" CJ asked as he walked toward the bed I was laying in. Glancing quickly at the clock and back at the window, I rolled my eyes. I knew for sure that, at 7:30pm, he wasn't coming to tell me that he would be staying in tonight. As I listened to the music from afar in the living room where the kids and friends were gathered, I took in several deep breaths before answering and released them with sigh, knowing what he was he was about to tell me. As he kissed me on my forehead three times back to back, he told me that he was about to make some moves and he would see me soon. The inner me could only hope and pray that God would bring him home once again. As the six-foot-three, eighteen-year-old boy that I fell madly in love with raced down the hallway to catch up with his homies, I asked God to spare his life, not knowing my family would be doing the same for me only hours later.

Well, the kids are in the living room. I may as well take a nap, and maybe when I wake up, he will be standing beside me telling me he made it in, I thought as I repositioned my body, seeking a little more comfort. At least, that's what always happened in the past. Just at the peak of finding some sort of sleep, footsteps of a hysterical yet calm voice intruded on what was supposed to be a nap, forcing me to get out of bed.

"Reshon! Reshon, get up, bro, we gotta go!" Kia said. I couldn't quite piece together what was happening, but I remembered to always go with the flow and ask questions later. I moved swiftly down the hallway, trying to think positive in yet such an adrenaline rushed time. I grabbed Elijiah, my son, who was one at the time, and Kia grabbed Isaiah who was four.

"What's going on?" I kept asking, as myself and 5 others loaded into a maroon Suburban.

Kia hopped in the driver's side, mashing the gas to pull us out of the garage that was pushed back due to old concrete that was coming up. She hopped out of the truck again to close the garage door that could only be opened from the inside. I glanced back to see my mother-in-law buckling in my oldest son and with another kid, reassuring them that everything would be okay.

I firmly locked my fingers right at Elijiah's waist, whispering, "Mama's got you, baby," as Kia jumped back into the truck.

Immediately after pulling out of the driveway and onto the dark misty road, she put a little extra force that soon plunged the truck forward. Trying to process what was occurring, I vividly recalled hearing about a phone call received stating that the house would soon be shot at. With everything happening so fast, my intuition kicked in, causing me to side-eye the rearview mirror. Looking out, I saw a white Grand Marquise with dark tinted windows speeding to catch up with us. When we reached the end of the street, we hit the corner, causing the truck's tires to screech. That's when I realized we were being chased, and it wasn't for fun.

Grabbing my son tighter, I said, "Go down highway 30 so we can go to my mom's house. They won't find us there. They will lose us!" I then pressed one on my phone to bring up my mom's contact info. As of today, I feel the safest place in the whole wide world, outside of the presence of the most high God, is being near my mom. I repeated for her to take my instructions and go to my mom's house as she became more nervous. As the car became closer, it seemed as if rain began to fall harder.

"Oh my gosh, I can't see!" she yelled.

What could I have done differently that would have avoided me being in this heart racing situation? Perhaps listened to my mom when she warned me not move in with my boyfriend. Or should I feel like this is all a dream that I could soon wake up from? These were some of the smaller thoughts that came to me as I realized that this was reality. With Kia slowly losing control of the car, right before we crashed, I whispered, "No, no, no!"

"Lay down, baby. Lay down," Kia told Elijiah as she used her body as a shield of protection from the heartless chasers ignoring the fact that her body was pinned down to the crushed vehicle by the seatbelt. Street lights beamed down on my soon to be unconscious body as people opened their door, calling 911 in disbelief. Grunting and grasping for air, I landed face down in the mud after being ejected out of the front window. We'd crashed into a pole and a tree.

Growing up, I always said that I would have my mom on

speed dial with the idea that she would come save me. Except, this night, March 25th, she had to witness hearing the life of her daughter leaving her body when she reached her voicemail calling to come home.

CHAPTER TWO

"We're losing her! We're losing her," the many doctors exclaimed as they shuffled their feet, rushing me through the double doors of the OR. As my mom and her supporters prayed the prayer of faith and protection, my family grew eager and worried as they learned of all the life-threatening injuries I had suffered. Among my injuries included a broken collarbone, fluid surrounded both my heart and lungs, several broken ribs, and there was brain swelling. In the doctors' eyes, I was almost completely lifeless.

As time passed, my vitals began to take a turn for the worse, pushing the doctors to wake my mom up at 2am with more hurtful news, as if she hadn't already received enough. "Mrs. Wesley, she isn't getting any better. She is in critical condition, and I think it's best to get the family here to see her for the last time," the doc advised her a few times, being that I was resuscitated three times mechanically.

My children were released from the children's hospital to my parents, who would care for them if I were to pass, which at this time it was expected. Elijiah suffered from a broken arm, and Isaiah suffered mentally from seeing his mom being thrown out of a window not knowing if she was alive. Sometimes, I have to wonder if mental injuries are more intense than physical.

"I Need Thee" is an old church hymn that church members sang as they gathered together holding hands around what many thought would be my death bed. With expectations of God showing up, they stood firm, believing in His word that, "Where two or more are gathered together in thy name, I am in the midst"—Matthew 18:20. Daily prayers and readings filled the Intensive Care Unit as the waiting room eventually reached maximum capacity, the vast majority of those bodies belonging to my friends and family. One by one, they would come in, only to break down to my swollen, cold body with tubes entering and exiting all over, with no response from me.

"Who did my sister's hair like this? Reshon, we have to talk about these toes," my brother would tell me as he tried to soothe over this moment for everyone. Mario is the jokester of the family, and he has a theory that if he can make you laugh about a situation, it will be alright soon. Still fighting back the urge and anger, he hesitated to ask who caused this devastating accident. He was would catch the bus to Baylor Medical Center in Dallas, night after night, just to sleep in the waiting area as many others made sacrifices to be with me at that time.

Each day my visitors increased, and it became overwhelming to me, at least that's what the staff thought. "Mr. & Mrs. Wesley, I am going to have to ask you to allow her some time to rest. All of the commotion from visiting is causing too much stimuli," the nurses would say.

Hanging on to the fact that she could be losing, yet again, another daughter, she went home to care for my boys, trying to stay prayerful. Mixed emotions from sadness to gratefulness filled her very existence. From receiving cards, flowers, food, and necessities to help with my boys, my mom still pressed forward knowing that there is a God. Jumping out of bed many sleepless nights, my mom would lay on the living room floor to hold my boys as they cried for me. While soothing and rocking them back sleep, she bellowed on the inside.

"Jereme is in a coma, and her survival rate right now is fairly low. We are doing all we can do to keep her comfortable." My nurses stated the medical term, yet in layman's terms, that meant they were keeping me comfortable until I died. Being told that if I survived I would be mentally impaired and unable to walk, my mom refused to accept any more bad news. She began a quest for answers from God regarding my healing and her peace.

"*God, I know that you can do all things, and I'm asking that you heal my daughter in your mighty name. No more pain. No more suffering. Lord, I'm giving it all to you! Heal her body as you did those in the bible! You said that you would be our doctor in the sick room, and Lord, we are here because we need your healing! Lord, we are no longer believing the reports of the doctors. Your reports are credible, so we so we are believing the reports of the Lord! From this day forward, no doctor will call me with any more bad news! I speak for perfect sleep and peace. In your mighty name, we pray. AMEN!*"

CHAPTER THREE

LYING in bed on a four-point restraint, with left and right chest tubes to drain fluid, receiving nutrients through a feeding tube, and depending upon the ventilator to breathe for me, I somehow woke up. Not physically but internally.

"Has the patient in room B had a feeding?" a passing nurse asked one of her colleagues.

Wait, wait! Who, me? I thought as I mentally tried to raise myself up to clear up the confusion. *Let me go over and tell them they have the wrong person. I'm just here because of an asthma flare-up.* Words from the inside. Attempting to move again, I went nowhere. *Come on, Reshon. Get up!* I continued to tell myself while fighting on the inside to move the heavy weight that was tying me to the bed.

"Give her four milligrams," the nurse ordered. As they finished up, they walked out and turned off the lights. Here I was, alive on the inside and dead on the outside. *Okay, this has to be a dream.* I began imagining myself escaping as a result. I envisioned myself crawling to the end of the bed, looking around to make sure no one saw me. It was dark, and there were other hospital beds that had lifeless bodies on them all around me.

Looking ahead across the room, I saw a few bodies that appeared to be dangling in all white in the air. *Angels? In the hospital? Ahhh, nah, I have to go! I will just go outside and stand on the bus stop because my surroundings look so familiar, so I know where I'm at. I'll go home to my mom and children. It's safe there.*

I was still neglecting the fact that my flesh laid there in that hospital bed approaching death, and all of this was just my imagination. Again, my inner-me created this plan that was so impossible being in a comatose body but it felt so real. I envisioned myself out on the street waiting for the bus to come in my hospital gown with an IV hanging from my arm. I kept looking around, making sure no one would see and try to bring me back into the place where they mistakenly tried to keep me. Or, at least, that's what I thought. With all of this imagining going on, my medicine began wearing off, and I started coming out of the coma they were trying to keep me in. After the last round from the nursing staff, I was now sitting up halfway in the bed. With my eyes barely open, the nurse came in and spoke to me.

"Hi, do you know where you are?"

After I nodded my head yes, he preceded to ask me where. With all of the scarring in my throat, I had no voice to speak, but I tried softly. "In the nursing home."

"Okay, do you know what month we are in?" He waited for me to provide the wrong answer.

But again, in the quietest voice, I managed, "April."

He reassured me I hadn't completely lost it by praising me for that right answer. Once again, he left me in the room, and I noticed my hands were no longer restrained and my legs were a little loosened. Glaring downward, I noticed the tubes from what seemed like were in my gown. I began to pull on them, and they grew longer and longer and then, eventually, bloody. Bursting in from behind the curtains, the nurse rushed over to the side of the bed, forcefully laying me down.

"You are *not* supposed to pull on these. Ugh," He aggressively shoved the tubes back up my nose while calling for more meds to be brought in by another nurse. I see why they tell medical professionals not to treat unconscious patients any kind of way, but believe it or not, some of us remember. By this time, I'd been in the ICU for a week or a little more. Things began to happen that the doctors couldn't believe, such as me breathing on my own since I had lung failure. Medical professionals were coming in and out of the room and would talk to me as I sat in somewhat of a daze.

Using the call light button, I called my nurse because I wanted to use the phone. I wanted to know who left me there. I needed answers to where my kids were, and also, where my boyfriend was. I called my mom, and hearing her voice brought tears to my eyes. "Mom, I want to come home."

She said in the sweetest voice, "You can't, baby. You've got to get to better, okay? Mommy loves you, and I'm praying for you."

Sitting there staring into space, I still didn't understand what was going on, nor did I bother to ask. I heard a voice that sounded like my daddy's voice, so I glanced down and under the curtain where I saw cowboy boots. My heart smiled, but still, I had no facial expression.

"Hey, baby! You know who I am?" He looked at me with his bloodshot red eyes, indicating that he was tired. He asked again, "You know who I am?"

I started nodding my head yes as I had been doing to everyone who had questions for me. My dad asked me if I knew what was going on, sort of assuming that I didn't. He told me that I had been in a car wreck, and I giggled a little, not thinking he was serious. He repeated himself to let me know that this was almost the end of my life. When I asked for my mom yet again, he told me she was at home with the kids. They didn't allow them to see me as much due the condition I was in.

Sinking down in the bed, I started to feel like my mom was mad at me. I suddenly heard a deep voice.

"Hey, Mr. Wesley." Carlton, my boyfriend, had walked in. After not seeing him in what felt like several weeks, or least while I was in a prolonged sleep, I didn't have much to say to him. I looked at him and rolled my eyes as if I knew he had done something that wasn't right. "I love you, baby. I'll be back," he said, something I was used to hearing from him, yet I had little to no strength to pray for his safe return.

"Dad, they haven't fed me." Unbeknownst to me, I wasn't taking solids yet. My dad asked the nurse what would be appropriate for me to eat, and she said she would call down to the cafeteria because of my special diet. Several moments later, the nurse returned with a black tray that had two bowls, a cup, and a straw in the middle.

"Dad, if you would feed this to her slowly and call us if there is a reaction, that would be great," the nurse said before rushing off quickly.

Looking at the side of my dad's head, I whispered, "I don't want that." Telling me in so many words that I didn't have a choice, he slowly put the spoon up to my mouth, and after a few bites, I didn't want anymore.

I was okay as long as someone was there with me and they could witness what was going on, but that also had to come to an end. As a little girl, I remembered my daddy pulling his pants up on one side and then on then other, which always meant that he was about to leave wherever we were. "I'm about to get back on the road. I've been off for some time now, remember?" At this point, I didn't remember coming into these four curtains that I can seem to escape, so to answer your question, *no*, I thought. Coming closer to my bed railing, my dad looked me in my eyes and told me not to talk to anyone that may come into the room asking questions. Looking confused, he clarified that I needed to make it known that I had a lawyer already and needed not to speak unless he was present.

CHAPTER FOUR

I WAS FINALLY MOVED into a regular room, and at this point, I felt regular, too, outside of the chest tubes and catheters that were still in place. New faces came in to introduce themselves, which I felt the slightest relief for. I kept thinking to myself, *When will that one special person come in to tell me what is really going on?* No one showed to fulfil my request. I soon learned that I would need therapy to learn to walk again, and the lady who would be doing it was fairly sweet. After she wrote her name on the board, I asked for pain medicine because I just wanted to sleep. As if I hadn't slept long enough already. The nurse came with water and the pill, reiterating what the physical therapist had told her. After I swallowed the pill, she told me to get some rest, and as she walked toward the door she dimmed the light.

I was just barely getting into the sleep I needed when I heard Kia's voice. "Ressssshhoooonnn, oh my gosh, I am about to cry!" I smiled so hard at her, probably the hardest I'd smiled in a while. "I can't tell you enough how happy I am that you are alive. Has anyone told you what happened?" I told her no one had and begged her to tell me, but she begged me not to drag her down memory lane and preferred to discuss it when I was better. "I don't want to upset you right now," she said, holding my hand. I asked her where Carlton was, and being considerate, she told me, "He will be back. You just need to rest." I dozed off on her a few times, so she insisted that she leave and come back later, and I was quite okay with that because the morphine had just settled in.

Falling into a deep sleep, I startled myself with a deep cough, one that was very painful might I add. Continuing to cough, I woke up in severe pain, feeling like I was being poked continuously. I called for my nurse because the severity of the cough started to worry me. Waiting on her to arrive, I took a look in my gown and noticed that there were staples holding an incision together in the middle of my chest, right between my breasts and descending toward my ribs.

"It's probably pain from your incisions. On a scale of one-to-ten, how severe is your pain?" she asked, washing her hands to give me pain relief. I had a pericardial window procedure done to help release all of the fluid on my heart that was causing it stop. I think it dawned on me then that my life had taken a turn for the worse and there was no coming back. *Is God mad at me?* Not bothering to give much thought into it, I blew it off and didn't bother to pray.

Brought up in a strict religious home, where prayer was the key to everything, I still didn't quite believe at this moment that He would hear me. Up until this point, I had been disobedient to both my parents and to God. "Honour thy mother and thy father that thy days may be long upon the land which the Lord thy God giveth thee." Exodus 20:12. A commandment that I oh so faithfully recited every Sabbath from a little girl to a young lady, I eventually ignored the fact that I still needed to adhere to Gods requests. But why would God do this to me? I mean, would He deliberately make me suffer? At least, I thought I was suffering from just the little that I knew about. Or had He removed his hand of protection over my life, allowing things to happen to grasp my attention because of my evil ways? I didn't kill anyone, well, not physically. I never committed adultery but fornicated on a regular basis. My parents were pastors and ministers, and sometimes, I felt it was necessary to live up to what people in society said about preachers' kids. I actually thought it was kind of cool because we stood out. They said we were fast, disobedient, and a more common word to sum up being good in bed, we were 'freaks.' Or was this just Satan's way of wheeling his way into our lives by making us think people really cared about who we were and our existence? "Satan comes to kill, steal, and destroy." John 10:10. He doesn't care who he uses, as long as they are willing to succumb to his offerings. But, then again, did their covering mean my siblings and I were all covered, too? *I need answers!*

Emotions raged, tugging at my heart. I felt all alone until my pastor walked and I awakened from the thoughts and the excuses I'd tried to bury myself in to exit reality. Not saying much but acknowledging that God is good, he stood on the side of the bed and held my hand. Inquiring about everyone in the family, I avoided making eye contact to keep from breaking down. Minutes passed to where, soon, he would have to leave as well, meaning I would be alone again. I can admit one of the most hurtful things I encountered was being left at the hospital by myself. What was I supposed to do in this idle and what felt like isolated time? Call on Jesus, perhaps? In the state of mind of where I could see nothing but helplessness, I steered my mind in the direction of how and when to get out of what I was in, as I was always good at getting myself out of things.

Another day passed, and a doctor came by just to remind me of how lucky I was to be alive. "We almost lost you. You've got to be more careful and be sure you wear your seatbelt," he told me, following that with information that explained the chest tube removal that he would soon perform so I could start physical therapy.

Self-reflection: You mean to tell me you didn't wear a seatbelt either, Reshon! At such a time like that, a seatbelt was the least of my worries.

Interrupting my one on one with myself, my kids, my mom, my sisters, my aunts, and my cousin all walked in, not to mention they traveled from Louisiana to see me. Everyone hugged me very lightly, trying not to brush up against all of my equipment. Elijiah and Isaiah stared at me in fear."

Come here, baby," I called for them, but they refused. I hadn't seen myself in the mirror yet to know that I had gotten skinny and my pupils were dilated from all the trauma and medication I had been through. My kids were scared, and at that age couldn't piece together the emotions to show or feel at that time. The last time they had seen me was when we wrecked. Laughter and talk filled the room until it was time for them to leave. Embracing everybody one by one, I felt a lump in my throat, wanting to plead with them to stay.

After asking for my medicine again so I could sleep off my unease, I looked at the clock. It was almost 12am. My room was upstairs, so my view was of the top of the building with smoke coming from it and nothing else but darkness. It reminded me of that place I was in not too long ago, a place where no one wants to be.

The next morning started off a little better than others because it was tube removal day. "Take a deep breath in and hold until I say release," the surgeon instructed me as he did both the right and the left lung. He took both of the chest tubes that were inserted into my lungs and connected them to a collection chamber that retained all of the fluid drained. I asked him when I would be able to go home, and he told me, "Hopefully, within the next week." I missed Easter that year; although, I had never really been into what was, in my eyes, a pagan holiday. Somehow, I remembered that it was around this time we celebrated Passover.

Hours later, it was time for me to try to walk again, and my therapists arrived to assist with that. Standing in front of me with a gait belt, the physical therapist told me what to do. Learning to walk from a baby seemed so much easier than as an adult. Pulling up with the dead weight of my legs that had been immobile for weeks now was very trying, but I was determined. When we stepped out into the hallway, there was a walker waiting on me. The therapist proceeded to the other end of the hallway, while another one stood near me against the wall with a wheelchair in case I fell.

"I want you to walk toward me slowly, and if you feel yourself getting tired, let me know, okay?" she said loudly. After pushing a walker, something that I had seen before in my class that mainly elderly individuals used, I became emotional. I was hurting. I wasn't strong enough mentally, emotionally, or physically to bear the weight that was on me, but I pressed on. Dragging one foot after the other, with tears in my eyes, I made it to the end of the hall. She smiled and applauded me on the progress but wasn't aware that, deep down inside, I wanted to give up and wished I would've given up on that operating table. She instructed me to walk back to the room, and I told her that it hurts, but she said something that has stuck with me right until this day. "I know it's painful, but you've got to keep going." No matter how hard life gets, no matter how immobile you feel due to the weight of your problems, you've got to keep going. Pushing past your pain will strengthen that durability you have built to uphold who you have become. I made it back into the room where she gave the option of sitting in a chair for a little while or lying back down. I chose to sit. How much worse could it get before I reached out to the man who could change this all? I decided it was time to surrender.

"*Lord, if you are there, I need your help right now! This is all too much for me. You said you wouldn't put more on me than I can bear, but I feel defeated! I feel helpless like my hands are tied. I know I've always taken things into my own hands, but I'm sorry, Lord, for all that I've done! For all of the lies I've told, all of my vindictive ways, all of my ill feelings, I'm sorry! Take them away from me and create in me a new heart. I want to be more like you. I can't make it on my own. I need your healing, Lord. You kept me here for a reason, so I'll say yes, Lord! Yes, Lord, to your will. Use me in any way you see fit. I'm not sure what happened, but put me in a place to where I don't just see this as a tragedy, so I can use it as a testimony! In your mighty name, AMEN!*

CHAPTER FIVE

"Do you know who will be picking you up today, Ms. Wesley?" the morning shift nurse asked me. I had no idea, and I didn't care how I got home as long as I got there. I called my mom and asked her to come get me. Man, to be back in Mom's presence was to die for, let alone seeing my children again. She couldn't leave because she was the daycare provider for kids and couldn't load them all up, but she arranged for some members of the church to pick me up. My excitement grew as I prepared to go home.

The pain intensified as the hour passed by, and my point to be medicated was soon to be cut off. The nurse brought in a wheelchair, and then I knew it was real. Having not seen daylight for three or four weeks was one of the hardest things ever. I felt trapped. The nurse came in with discharge papers, and my soul rejoiced. *I made it! Lord, you did it! You heard me!* Still holding my composure on the outside, slumped over with no ribs for support, I nodded to the instructions she gave me to survive from that point forward. Slowly getting in the chair, it hit me that God hadn't forgotten about me. By this the time, my ride had arrived, and the hospital transporter was pushing me past the nurses' station. All of the "you are lucky" wishes filled the halls all the way to the elevator. "Ground Floor", I heard in my ear from the automated elevator voice, but for some reason, everything else zoned out. I heard nothing. Still going, we finally reached outside and all I could do was look.

"She may be a little out of it for a while. Give her some time," the transporter said, and I assumed someone asked me a question and I didn't respond.

Making a right out of Baylor Medical Center to head my mom's house, I looked around in amazement at the sun, the flowers, all of the passing cars, the houses, just the existence of what God had created. I instantly had a new appreciation for life and everything that was in it. Still amazed at how beautiful everything was, we pulled up to Mom's house. I started crying because that's all I had been asking for, was to just be with my mom. I got in the house, where I hadn't really spent much time since I moved out.

As I got I settled in, it felt as if the pain began to get worse. Walking with assistance to the couch, I asked my mom to call in my pain medication to Wal-Mart. I smelled the sweet scent of Lysol, and I knew that she had cleaned and re-arranged for me to come home. When I was fifteen, I delivered my first child. I would call my mom while I was in the hospital, crying to go with her. She couldn't come each time I called, and I wasn't sure why, but I knew it wasn't anything personal. When Isaiah and I got home, everything was cleaned and rearranged for our arrival, and for every child after, she did this gracious act for me. Each time, it reminded me that with God, no matter how far you go, no matter what you do, you can still come home and God will accept you with open arms, because His love is unconditional and never ending.

My right collarbone was broken, and my arm was severely injured. My arm was so heavy, I kept my shoulder tensed up to help with the pain. There was a big cut from me bursting through the glass that my mom would clean and dress with gauze for me. One of the first things I knew I wanted was to take hot bath when I got home, but I knew I couldn't do it alone. "When all of the kids leave, I'll get you in the tub," she told me, having no problem bathing her nineteen-year-old daughter because I couldn't myself. Sitting in the tub slumped over, my mom would sit on the toilet on the side of the tub and wash my back in awkward silence. I know she did this when I was a baby, but I was gown now. Well, at least, that's what I thought. I wish I had that fight in me as I did on my sick bed to my bathe myself, but the fact of the matter is I really needed my mom. This sort of brought me to the point that sometimes God will bring us down to a level where we have no other choice but to fall in total submission unto Him because we need Him more than anything.

Later that day, I went into the living room to rest on the couch, and it's almost like my mom knew that something was on my mind besides almost losing my life. She reassured me that my school knew everything that had occurred, so my attendance and grades were okay. I attended Remington College for my certification as a Medical Assistant and carried a 4.0 grade point average. I made great decisions in school but bad ones in life.

I had received my cell phone, that was somehow in perfect condition, back in the hospital; I just didn't have any interest in going through it during my torturous stay. Before clicking on anything, I remembered that my phone may have been handed down from a few people, and it wasn't suitable for anyone to go through. What if everyone had all passed my phone around? That means they saw all my nudes that I had unashamedly taken, or the conversations between a guy and I from Louisiana who I lied to and conned him out of money often by telling him I needed it to come where he was but never showed up. He would send money out of his hard-earned check every week for every sob story that I so creatively told him. At times, I'd even run outside to make it seem like I was stranded on the side of the road on the way to see him seven hours away. All the while googling intersections to give him some type of certainty that I was really coming, and then somehow conveniently there was a western union or a Walmart near where I could receive what he was sending to me. Karma maybe? Or was this all me reaping what I had sowed? The bible never gave a specific timing or description on this concept, but I do understand that what you put in is what you will get out. Whether it's tomorrow or years down the line, always remember to "Do unto others what you would have them do unto you." Luke 6:31.

Still staring into space, I eventually snapped out of it and proceeded to go through the phone. Text messages from everyone rolled in before my data could fully kick in. One of the text messages were from some girls in my class who disliked me for an unknown reason and pretty much made my days in class awkward by staring and making snide comments. "Sorry we ever treated you like that. We just want this all to be over,". Another said, "In case I never told you, I love you." Many others received were prayers that I would wake up. I then went to Facebook where similar posts circulated my page. My sister, Shunta, captured memories in the form of pictures, just in case the doctor's word of my memory loss were to come to pass. My first visitors when I got home were my classmates, surprisingly. They came with cards that everyone at the school had signed for me, and they brought my favorite food that we always ate at lunch together, Taco Bell. I guess this would've been a good time to clear the air as to why I was mistreated, but the new me wouldn't allow my mind to take that route. While thinking that the last thing they said to me wasn't right, I'm sure they ate their actions and words at the thought of losing someone without the chance of apologizing. Lesson learned to be mindful of the things you do and say to people.

For months, all I was able to do was lie around with the perfect time to think about this life that God gave me another chance at. Every day, I had the love and support from family and friends to help get me through this rough time. Night times became the worst due to flash backs I started having. One night, I fell into a deep sleep and all I heard was glass shattering, gunshots, and sirens. I woke up out of my sleep needing and wanting God to hold me at that time. I sat on the side of the bed staring into the hallway that led to the living room. It was dark, something I became afraid of at that time. Finding the strength, I pulled myself up and walked to my mom's room. She turned over as soon she felt me standing behind her. "Mom I'm sorry for everything I put you through, and thank you for taking care of me and the boys," I cried and fell into her arms. I couldn't imagine her explaining to my children that their mom had passed away.

CHAPTER SIX

I woke to the smell of homemade biscuits on the morning that I would be meeting with Child Protective Services. Me? CPS? This doesn't even go well with my name at all! Those were the thoughts that continued to circulate in my mind as I grew angrier with each minute that passed, along with many others. At some point or another, I was told that Carlton had turned himself in. I wasn't sure why, but this added to the weight I was carrying. Sitting on the couch in confusion as to why this would be happening to me, I heard the doorbell ring.

A tall, slim woman with a black briefcase entered, looking around to see the environment my children were living in. She invited me to sit at the kitchen table with her so we could talk. After introducing herself, she asked, "Do you know why I'm here?" As a defense mechanism, I wanted to snap her head off but I didn't.

"No," I told her, looking at the papers she was pulling out. She explained to me that they were contacted by the children's hospital due to Elijiah and Isaiah being brought in the night of the wreck, and it was told that the wreck was caused by a violent situation. Watching my body movements, she had her pen in hand and paper ready to write down anything she could that didn't sit well with her.

"Do you remember what happened on the night of the wreck?" I couldn't tell her exactly because I still didn't know what happened, just by word of mouth that I was in a wreck. "So, you're telling me you don't remember anything?" she asked, insinuating that I was not telling the truth. It was obvious she didn't get the memo that I was in a coma and at that time was experiencing short term memory loss.

"Ma'am, I don't remember anything as of now."

She began to ask me a series of question about my boyfriend. "Where was Carlton on the night of wreck?" Again, with not too much of an answer, I stuttered, telling her that he'd gone to the store. It wasn't that I wasn't telling the truth; I just wasn't sure where all this was coming from and I still hadn't spoken to him. "Look, I want you to understand that this situation is serious, and as a result, your children could possibly be removed from your home." I started tearing up just hearing that my boys could possibly be taken from me, the most injurious thing a mother could encounter. "You told me that you didn't know what happened that night, now you are saying he was at the store. Which one is it?" She presented her questions in a very interrogating manner and continued to badger me with questions about this situation that I wasn't very knowledgeable about with no remorse. She started asking me about weapons that he owned and asked me if I owned any. "So, you are unaware that Carlton drove by another individual's home and shot at them, grazing a child?" Complete silence had overtaken me at that time. Still not able to put anything together, the visit had come to an end. She gave me instructions to follow. "You nor your children are allowed to be around Carlton until the investigation is complete. You all are not allowed to go near the home. He isn't allowed to come around you all, and if these rules are broken, this will result in automatic removal." After handing me her card, she walked off.

Why does this woman think I would hurt my children, or even put them in harm's way for that matter? I sat at the table for a moment, and I remembered my mom teaching us that the decisions you make in life will not only affect you but will affect those around you. Days passed with the thoughts of losing my children, which continued to break me more than I already was. I was told that I could pass custody down to my parents if anything were to come out of this. Part of me was comforted by that, but a larger part of me was questioning God. I almost lost my life, and now could potentially lose my children. *What am I really here for?* My existence would have no meaning due to everything that held significant value in my life being taken away.

I finally made arrangements to where I was able to get in contact with Carlton. I was anxious and a little scared to hear the real story as to what happened. My brother continued to tell me that had I not lived, Carlton would've suffered. With just that piece of information, I knew it couldn't have been good, but I also knew he wouldn't do anything to hurt me or our children.

After coming home, several people suggested that I leave him alone, but they never gave a reason to solidify their pleading. As far as I was concerned, he didn't do anything to me. For the most part, my parents were not telling me this, so I didn't care to listen to the opinions of others. "You have a collect call from Carlton Sparks." My phone couldn't have been picked up any faster.

"Baby! What happened?! Where are you?!" I wanted to be mad at this point, but I was relieved just to know that he was okay. He wouldn't tell me much because the calls were recorded, but I explained to him that CPS was now involved in our lives.

"I need you to tell me the truth. Did you shoot at those people's house?" I asked, wanting answers to every question.

He said that he didn't do that and I believed him. "Reshon, call my lawyer, and if anyone else asks, I didn't do it."

I went with it and got in contact with his lawyer. After

speaking with the lawyer, where the stories began to sound fishy. After he asked me to tell him what I knew, he advised me not to say anything else if I wasn't sure what happened, and taking his advice, I said nothing else. I started feeling as if I had been hit directly by a car with all of the extra stress I had taken on.

"You are doing too much! You need to rest," my family fussed at me because I just couldn't sit still after I discovered I could move around a little. A month passed and I decided that I was in good enough shape to go see him in jail. I had to pep-talk myself into doing this because of the conditions of the jail. Still not having healed all the way, I pressed my way down there. I walked up to the line where people gathered to see their loved ones. I started feeling faint, dizzy, and a little pain but I fought through it. After making it up to the floor he was on, my happiness excused the pain. I sat in the chair waiting for him to come to the window, not sure what his reaction was going to be. He walked through door and grabbed the phone before he sat down.

"Man." Dropping his head, he expressed how grateful he was that I'd made it through.

"Carlton, what happened?" He began to tell me, and the more I listened, the more things started to make sense to me. "Tell me the truth. Did you shoot at those people's house?" I had a gut feeling that he did, and he confirmed it. He told me that he did, then looking me in my eyes, he began to cry. "Why? You got me out here, lying, looking dumb. What were you thinking!?"

He told me that the guys who chased us had broken into the truck that his deceased dad had passed down to him. His passing had happened a little over four months prior to the accident which influenced his actions.

The visit became too much for me, and when I got home late that evening, I was hurting, not only physically but emotionally as well. At this point I felt as if I was losing me and everything that is a part of me. I might no longer have my children, the person I loved was gone away, and maybe for a while, I was weak with no more fight in me to push any further. Wouldn't it have just been easier for me to let go? Couldn't I have just passed and none of this would be affecting me? Did He leave me here so I could suffer? Selfish feelings coming from someone who didn't recognize that God didn't bring me this far to leave me. This test that I was put through was meant to become a testimony so others can see that God stays true to His word.

I pulled myself together to go to church that Saturday. Many of the members hadn't seen me since I was in the hospital. As soon as we pulled onto the church grounds, tears of happiness fell. The feeling of being in God's presence again, the sweet feeling of knowing that God made death behave on my behalf, and now I had the opportunity to give Him the Glory for it overcame me. By the time I walked into the house of the Lord, I was sobbing. While being embraced with hugs, I felt the depletion of fear. The fear that they would never see me again vanished, and the anticipation made itself known. Once again, God proved himself to be God.

Shockingly, there are non-believers who don't think or know that He is real. So, the almighty uses perfect situations such as mine as an opportunity to present himself to lost souls. Even with all of the welcoming gestures, I still felt empty on the inside, a feeling I knew all too well. As a child going into my teen years, I attended church every Friday and Saturday, and I sat on the front pew with high expectations that the word would mysteriously fall upon me. I recall the saying, "When you leave here today, don't leave the same," meaning the word that was brought forth should be good enough to change who you are or where you are with Christ. All of that good word, and still nothing was retained on the inside except emptiness. You have to have the desire to be filled with everything God has to offer and allow him to fill you up, which will lead you to restoration. All you have to do is ask and it shall be given unto you; seek and you shall find, Matthew 7:7. I guess I was too distracted with the things of the world and finding everything in it which filled me up while still leaving me void.

I was just as excited to see everyone but didn't know how to show it. After the word went forward, my presence was acknowledged again. Normally during testimonies, I would get emotional, just enough to shed a tear and say thank you to Jesus. Fact of the matter is He needs more than that. He wants all of us. Our good and bad, the things we think we are hiding from everyone else, He sees them all. He wants to take those very things that have been our prisons and set us free from them. In order for this to take place, it is imperative that we allow him to take full control of our lives. Sitting there hearing them say that I'm a miracle and explaining how the doctors were saying I was trying to die, came to me that maybe this was a reconstruction of my life. I survived what could have potentially killed me in the long run, my flesh. Sometimes, things happen to gain our attention when we have gone astray. All of the smaller hurdles weren't there to pull me down but to build me up with resilience, enabling me to withstand the world as I walk in my purpose. It was time for me to stop running from God and be the vessel that he needed me to be.

My mom always reminded my siblings and I how we all had callings in our lives, and what made it so believable was that we would always get prophesized to. There were instances where He tried to get my attention and did so through dreams. He will send some of the most unlikely people to let you know that you have work to be done.

I began to shake my leg to the fast-paced music that brought upon a shout from many others. I couldn't give him the praise physically like I wanted to, so I began to call on his name. "God, you loved me enough to save my life. All of my dirt, all of my insecurities, me shaming your name, and you left me here. I'm sorry, God. I'm sorry!" This all flowed from my mouth, allowing His power to transform me in the midst of me praising Him for what he had done for me. That cup on the inside that was once filled by the world was now filled with grace and new life.

"Now may the God of hope fill you with joy and peace and believing, that you may abound in hope by the power of the Holy Spirit," Romans 15:13. It was something about everything that was occurring at that time that made me realize that all of it had to have been for a reason. Whether it was God gaining all of the glory for bringing me out or molding me to be victorious through every obstacle I would face, either way, He had a plan for me. "For I know the plans I have for you, plans to prosper you, and not to harm you, plans to give you hope and a future," Jeremiah 29:11.

"God, I don't know where to begin, but you know all things. I'm grateful for another chance you have given me, and now I understand why you left me here. I know that I can do all things through Christ who gives me strength, so I'm going to press forward. I know this won't be easy, and I know I'll make mistakes, but I ask you to order steps as I get back on track. Cover me and my family under your blood. In the mighty name of Jesus, Amen."

CHAPTER SEVEN

CHECKING the mailbox had become something I looked forward to daily, especially with my newfound confidence in God that he was going to turn that situation with child protective services around. There was still that mere thought of if they really took them from me, what would I do? Then there were times I would like to believe that maybe they forgot about the situation, as sometimes I wish I could. Weeks and weeks had gone by, and I'd still heard nothing. At that time, I felt like the person I was growing up when I prayed on something and it didn't happen right away. During this journey, I've learned that things happen on God's timing, and just because we don't get an immediate response doesn't mean He isn't working on our behalf.

"Dear Ms. Wesley, this letter is to inform you that the case filed with our office is now closed."

The letter I had been waiting on finally came, and right on time, too, because I was just about to give up. There will be plenty of times where you feel like throwing in the towel, and just as you are about to, God will step in to remind you that He hasn't forgotten about you. At this time, I felt like things were getting better with each day that passed. Going to the doctor after the accident was never easy because the fear of the unknown always tried to overpower me. I am a witness of God's power being greater than any fear, and I gained the ability to discharge those thoughts and feelings in the name of Jesus.

I started to see a change within myself the more I began to grow closer to God, but I knew He wasn't done with me yet. During the times I would be alone, there was something about the silence that filled the space that I occupied, and it was almost like I felt someone's presence there. I just couldn't pinpoint it. I couldn't help to think about how strange this quietude was, and how to react to it because I'd never felt it before. My mom would always tell me when we don't know what else to do, in whatever situation it may be, we were instructed to pray. These times began to happen more frequently, and I found it to be quite peaceful. Not knowledgeable of it at the time, I started praying and asking God to be with me, not knowing he was already there.

Growing up, I longed for that butterfly feeling in my stomach everyone talked about from their significant other. For some odd reason, I never really felt it, I just took what seemed like the flutter feeling and attached it to the description to help address my wants. God showed me that He can be everything I need and everything that I want. He topped that temporary sensation and gave me the internal peace that has a never-ending flow. I got used to that so I began to pray more, and not only when something was going wrong, which I was guilty of in the past. God isn't interested in our problems because He has already worked it out, but he is attracted to our praise, which in exchange he will send down answers to our problems and blessings for our patience. After my brother had taken me to the doctor for follow-ups a few times, I started going on my own. This proved the doctor's probability of the post-traumatic stress disorder label they tried to place on my life to be zero. On my last visit, I was having all of my incisions examined as well as an overall check-up up to receive clearance to go back to regular activities. I sat on the table as the doctor removed the gauze I had placed over my surgery sites.

"Ms. Wesley, I notice you have coverings over these wounds. Have you had any drainage or bleeding from them lately?" he asked moving on to the biggest incision that was completely healed in the middle of my chest. "You can let these breathe now. They are not as bad as they seem." Little did he know, he was providing me with further instructions on how to move forward from this tragedy and how to survive on this walk with Christ. In life, you will go through trials and tribulations in which some will leave you feeling severely wounded with just an ounce of strength left. That little bit of strength is meant to be used to reach out to God, for His strength is made perfect in our weakness. I was honestly left in awe at how God had healed my body in just that short length of time, which left me to question what else He could do. He said in his word that He is able to do exceeding, abundantly above all that we can ask or think.

Within the next few days, I knew I would start back school. This gave me a head start on the worrying, which I tried to reduce by praying. During this growing process, I've learned you can't worry and pray at the same time. I had given Him everything that I was carrying on my heart, and on my shoulders, and trusted Him. My smallest bit of faith gave me motivation to run on and let God handle the rest.

Within no time, I found myself sitting back at a desk in school doing what I was told I wouldn't be able to do. Coming back into class, I was treated differently. At least, that's how I felt. I was offered tutorials to refresh my memory on material and was often told if I needed anything repeated to make the instructor aware. Although, this did make me feel some type of way, I also had to remember that not everyone understands how God works, so it's important that we be that example. Regardless of everything I had been through, I still had memory of all previous work I had done, and my skills were still at a mastery level. *Well, why was it so hard to remember what happened from the wreck?* A question I had as well as many others. Anything that God gives us is precious and must be handled delicately so that its purpose is fulfilled. It is kind of like planting a seed in the ground with expectations of it growing beautiful and strong with the ability to withstand strong winds, being stomped on, and different weathers. Being that my situation was going to be used to help pull some people through, He couldn't just give it to me without growing me some more. I was that seed. I wasn't in a space mentally or spiritually to deliver what happened to me with the effect of saving lives. Although, as a seed, I went through the rough process of being buried in dirt, Him dusting me off time after time. I still had nutrients I needed to receive so that I could sprout out and blossom. The memory of what I endured slowly but surely came to me as God transformed me. I needed to be in the right place to tell you that there is nothing too hard for God.

CHAPTER EIGHT

THE MONTH OF OCTOBER APPROACHED, and it was time for a lot great things to happen for me. Just seven months ago, I was clinging onto machines fighting for my life, and now, momentarily, I would be on my way to making a better life for my children and myself. Carlton was due to get out soon, which also gave me a chance at building my family back up again. No one was nearly as excited as I was about him getting out besides our children. Plenty of family and friends went against the thoughts of us being back together because they wanted to blame him for everything I went through. I had grown mentally enough at that time to know that we can't blame things that we go through on everyone else, so I rejected their thoughts and opinions. Regardless of what anyone else felt, I forgave him. At least, I thought I did. I felt like this was the time for me to make a change for my family, especially if I had the power to do so. I began to make plans for us to move out of the city we were in once he was released.

The day arrived that I would be walking the stage and graduating from yet another school, which many doubted would happen. As I stood behind the curtain peeking out into the crowd, I had an instant flashback from childhood years, to teens, up until then, and I couldn't fathom how I was standing there about to make such a huge achievement. With all of the emotions raging, I almost missed my name being called to walk. "Jereme Wesley." My classmates cheered for me as I walked humbly onto the stage, and I heard my family yelling for me as well. That was one of the best times of my life, and I feel like those times tend to go by rather quickly while other times seem to linger. I was still in disbelief at what just took place and finally felt like I was actually progressing after that setback.

I applied for an apartment when I found out that he was coming home and was approved after graduation. Although, I'd built a relationship with God and started moving forward from a life changing situation, I still somehow managed to make decisions that were not the best for me. I began working for a gynecologist's office and was in a really great spot in my life. I had my children, they were well taken care of, my best friend was being released, and God was moving things. What else could I ask for?

I dealt with the guilty conscience at the thought of living with man that I wasn't married to, but I felt like God would excuse just this one thing because *He knew my heart*. I felt so convicted that I let up on my praying, falling back into fear that God was mad at me. Marriage was eventually a goal we wanted to achieve because we knew it is better to marry than to burn, but we just couldn't quite come together on one accord. I had the desire to live for Christ and do the right thing, yet he was heading in a completely different direction which caused us to clash. I began to anger inside with each day that passed because I felt like all of the work I put in, including the struggle I went through, started to become worthless. I couldn't understand why things were not going as I felt they should. One thing that I did fail to realize is that it is not our plans but God's, and when we get in line with Him, things will go a lot smoother. I kept trying to convince myself that God was looking at the better me and looking past the smaller things. At some point, I had begun to believe that, so I continued on with my ways that were not pleasing unto him. I had one foot in and one foot out with Him, which put me in a place to be susceptible and vulnerable to all the things the world had to offer.

As a child going through my primary school years, I was the child who always managed to get into some sort of trouble for doing things I knew I wasn't supposed to do. When my mom would speak with me, she asked why I had done that. Following behind her rhetorical question, she would advise me that I would be in more trouble because I knew better than to do some of the things I was doing. "For it had been better for them not to have known the way of righteousness, than, after they have known it, to turn from the holy commandment delivered unto them," 2 Peter 2:21. I knew this because of how I was raised, but I'd chosen to go another route.

Carlton and I continued to parent our children together, but things between us became rocky. Long nights of arguing and fighting became intense. There was glass throwing, door slamming, and sometimes even physical contact between us. "I almost died because of you!" One of the many hurtful things I would say often in the heat of things to try to reflect the hurt on someone else that I would later on regret. This was a sign that I still had work to do within myself, and I hadn't fully forgiven like I said I did. I began wondering if God was mad at me or if He'd had enough of me, or even if He was feeling like He did something so extreme for me to turn back and get back into some mess. That's the beauty of Him; God's love is never ending and He loves unconditionally. No matter how far you get in life, He is always there waiting with open arms.

We eventually came to the conclusion that this wasn't the best idea, regardless of how hard we fought to make it work. I prayed on this situation because it was hard. I wanted to be with him. I wanted my kids to experience the complete family, but we couldn't quite make it work. There were really good days, but the bad outweighed them. It took a lot of sleepless nights to understand that my life was not my own. Still being persistent on things that I wanted, I continued. I continued to be rebellious against what I knew was right. I was broken and couldn't see why, but never sought out healing from the only one who could do such a thing. I continued to look elsewhere except up high where my help came from. I know they say the tongue is powerful, but I felt the hurtful things I was saying to him weren't powerful enough to make him realize that I was hurting. I longed for comfort from the internal pain I was experiencing. I started doing things that were very vindictive, and the most damaging part was, it was done in front of our children.

I had enough one day and decided that I was done with all of the arguments, the disrespect, and just altogether I wanted out. I started throwing old wine bottles against the wall, knocking things off of the cabinet, and throwing his stuff out, too. One of the many fights I would start. After I felt like I had gotten my point across, I locked my door with the expectations of him not returning after he had left. I was in my room pacing because everything happened so fast. I hard three loud bangs, and I walked into the living room to my front door off the hinges. I couldn't believe that my door had just been kicked in by the person I loved, the person that said he loved me. But was love supposed to feel like this? He barged in and headed to the room to get the rest of his belongings, knowing that the police could possibly be called because of all of the commotion.

With my phone in my hand, trying to think clearly, my heart racing, hands shaking, everything came to a sudden stop. I tried to be okay with what just happened, but I was not. I was able to lift my door and put it back just enough to be safe. Contemplating on what I should do, I ended up calling maintenance, telling them someone kicked my door in and I needed immediate assistance. I was advised that I needed to make a police report, but I didn't. I hurried and cleaned the glass up that I destroyed and everything else that had been thrown on the floor so that the appearance of my apartment would match my story; someone tried to break in.

The kids finally fell asleep, and I was left alone with my haunting thoughts. I tried to bury the hurt with justification that this all was for my good. I found myself back on my knees needing God more than ever. I ran to Him for everything, and that's what He wants. We no longer need to fight our own battles because they don't belong to us. When we learn to give Him everything that may be hindering us from moving forward —pain, brokenness, insecurities, the feeling of abandonment— He will start to give us peace that surpasses all understanding, which also sets us free from situations that we never imagined coming out of.

From that day forward, I decided I have to go on and that I can no longer revive dead situations. I started praying and reading my bible again, but this time with my children. They had been through enough at an early age that all they needed was exposure to comfort. It was vital that I get back to that spot where I could focus on God and my children with knowledge that everything else was going to fall into place. I asked God to order my steps and to guide me in the right direction.

"God, this has been the hardest past few months for us, and I know I can go on, but I need you to help me! I want to get rid of all toxic things in my life and eliminate those things that aren't contributing to my evolvement in you and in life. God, I want to be what you called me to be, but I know I can't do that in the position that I am in and I can't do this alone. Lord, I need you more than ever! Help me to really forgive others in my heart, and if I hurt anyone, please allow them to forgive me. I want a release from feeling captive to my past and external things that have been pulling me down. I ask that you change the way I think so that I can be a better person. Give me the desire to want better for my children and myself. Please help me recover from this situation. I'm hurt but I know you heal. I'm broken and I know you mend, so I'm asking for your touch. Lord, I ask you all these things. In the name of Jesus, I pray, Amen."

Things between Carlton and I were off and on. I've learned

that the people we start off with in life won't necessarily be the people we end up with. That can be family, close friends, or even someone we consider to be our significant other. Why would we endure so much heartache and pain, and even conquer some of those tests together, just split and go our ways? That's hurtful, right? Well, during my storms, I held on and it hurt us more because I wasn't allowing God to work on us individually. Letting go of the past is essential for growth to take place. I couldn't see life outside of what I was used to, but remember that God will pull us out of our comfort zones to get us where we need to be.

CHAPTER NINE

GETTING out of bed became easier for me because of the change that was slowly taking place. I had a lot of reasons to be grateful, and I never wanted to take those for granted because every day isn't promised. After our big break-up, I felt like things were finally back on track. For sure, it wasn't how I really wanted it to go but definitely how it needed to go. I received a call from an employer whom I had applied for a little while back. I thought I wasn't qualified enough for it because I hadn't heard anything else from them. The call I received was a request for an interview with a recruiter for the E.R. in Presbyterian Hospital of Dallas. She began to tell me a little about the position and the requirements. She asked me about a nursing assistant certification, which I didn't have and that was the main requirement. I told her what I possessed, which was medical assistant certification. I automatically got a little discouraged but still proceeded with the interview in confidence. "Okay, Ms. Wesley, I'll pass this information on to the hiring manager, and if she wants to move forward, I'll call you again." I didn't put too much thought into it because I had already doubted anything would come out of that opportunity.

A day later, I got a call back stating that the hiring manager wanted to meet with me. I was excited but still had my guards up so that I wasn't disappointed if I didn't get it. "God, if this is for me, I ask that you allow me get the job and help me excel in it, amen." I decided to give to Him, that way it wouldn't become another worry of mine. I reminded myself that He wouldn't withhold anything good for me. Talking to Him on a regular basis became second nature to me. Weeks later, I had an interview with the manager and I felt it went well.

Before I left her office, I asked her in confidence, "When should I expect to hear from you?" From that moment, I began to claim things over my life, knowing that they would come to pass. I started making arrangements for how things would go for my children while I was working new hours. I decided this was a good time to finally speak with Carlton about co-parenting. We were not on speaking terms, so the only thing I could do is pray that it would go smoothly. I could tell a huge difference in our conversations, and when we spoke, tranquility was always present. I was almost always prepared to start yelling when we conversed about our children, but when I decided to let go and let God, my perception changed. Not only did I need Him to heal me physically, I needed him to heal me mentally so that I could move forward with clarity and focus on what was to come. I wasn't sure I would ever come to a place where I sincerely forgave the person whose actions almost cost me my life. How could I? A question that laid in my mind for so long until I got a clear vision of the power of forgiveness. It wasn't easy, but it was necessary.

When you ask God to do a new thing in you, and you stop allowing external influences to alter the inner you, things will start to shift. During this shifting period, things you didn't believe would happen will start to come to pass. When you fully forgive someone, chains that are holding you bound will break and freedom will reign over your life. All of the hatred, anger, hurt, betrayal, and anything that's causing you to want someone else to feel as wounded as you feel will no longer reside within you; what a wonderful feeling! I finally understood the importance of forgiving and why the bible pressed on it as hard as it did. Forgiving isn't for the other individual; it's for you! You can move forward without having that heavy burden on your shoulders which weighs you down and leaves you stranded in your past with no way of escape unless you forgive. It will cause you to miss out on many blessings, and it opens doors for the enemy to camp out in your life. Victimization will become your new mentality for everything that occurs in your life until you move forward and forgive. There are no limitations on this act. For it empowers others to follow this command so that they may also be released from confinement, mentally and emotionally, promoting their growth spiritually. He wants us to forgive as he has forgiven our sins. Ephesians 4:32, "and be ye kind one to another, tenderhearted, forgiving one another, even as God for Christ's sake hath forgiven you."

The revelation of God's divine healing started to take effect in every aspect of my life. Miracles and blessings continued to overflow right before my eyes as He promised. I received a call from the recruiter I spoke with initially.

"Mrs. Wesley, the manager wants to move on to the hiring process with you.. In shock, I asked her about the requirement that I didn't have. "She is going to extend your start date out, allowing you to go and get that other certificate you need." I felt the favor over my life immediately ensuring me that I was ready to step into my future. This transformation was like nothing I've seen before, none the less it didn't shock me that God would take full control over my life if I allowed him to.

NOW

My now had been laid out before me in the duration of my storms. Because God brought me out, I have a much clearer vision of my purpose. Victory and prosperity are the grounds that I walk on, and it is only because of God. I thought coming from such a life-threatening tragedy and so many hurtful situations that left my heart filled with affliction would be impossible, but God showed me that He specializes in transforming. Blessings continued to flow from many opportunities, to just waking up with a sound mind and being burden free. I had a choice, just as everyone else does, to allow my past to either make me or break me. I gained a new appreciation for life, causing me to cherish everything that came my way. Family, friendships, and even relationships, personal or professional, I learned to take something away from it that can later benefit me.

My thought process has taken a complete turn. I strive to take the positive out of every negative situation as I did with the car accident; I'm a miracle. Each scar I wear reminds me that I can get through each test that is assigned in my life. Many people find it hard to conceptualize the person I am today because of what I have been through, and honestly, I still do at times. I am currently fulfilling my dreams of empowering people to overcome every external obstacle that is blocking them from moving forward in their lives, most importantly moving forward in Christ. I find it quite amazing how God used what was meant for my bad and turned it into my good by instilling tools that I can now and later share with others to help them reconstruct their lives. After countless setbacks, shortcomings, and challenges, I didn't imagine myself overcoming, but my determination took a leap at the highest level. I would never tell you that this was a walk in the park, but what I will say is that choosing God to lead me has been the best decision I've made yet!

Have you chosen him? Choose ye this day whom ye will serve," Joshua 24:15. To be honest, this was the hardest decision because the thoughts of people walking away, the feeling of isolation because no one would understand me, or even just the fear of what lay ahead of me was what made it so difficult. Then, of course, I had to face reality of the other decision had I gone the other way of dealing with demons, devils, fear, curses, failure, unbreakable soul-ties, and more so, all of this by myself, because I'm chosen. And so are you! We can't do this alone. Your decision to explore more in depth of what God can and will do is just the beginning or the continuation of your journey in Christ. You will have those people who you would've never thought would have left your side, and there are times you will feel all alone, but you are not. He is with you every step of the way as He has been for me. How can I reach this level in God with an impure heart? What about my daily ways that shame his name? Even in the bible, they questioned about the plans He had for their lives and how to live. He said, "I am the way, the truth, and the life," John 14:5-6. These are questions I had before I really found my position in Christ, and they may even be a concern of yours, or even maybe someone you know is uncertain! I have a message for you. God died on the cross for our sins so that we can have eternal life. He loves us that much!

He forgives and all He needs is a willing heart that will open up and allow him to create a new thing within. 2 Corinthians 5:17, "Therefore if any man be in Christ, he is a new creature; old things are passed away; behold all things are become new."

Each day, he reminds me that His grace is sufficient and His mercy is new. Every day! Just that reminder itself gives me so much comfort and strength to run on, even on my worst days. Our situations and problems may be different, but the solution for us all is the same: JESUS.

I challenge you to build with Him, follow Him, and rely on Him for your every need. He has never failed me and won't fail you either. Every morning I wake up, He reminds me of how much He loves me by placing a song on my heart and reassuring me that He is all that I need, and He can do that for you, too.

I'm elated to be able to share my testimony with you. It took me a while to get here. When I realized that my story was not only for me, but for you, too, I couldn't hold it in any longer to let you know that you are coming out! Be blessed.

A PRAYER

A Prayer for you and me!

God, I come to you as humbly as I know how, thanking you for the chance you've allowed me to speak to your people. You did a mighty thing in my life and, God, I thank you. I don't know where I would be without you. Now that you have given me the power to speak over others, I'm asking you to guide them in the direction that they should go. I'm asking you to protect their hearts so that they would feel hurt no more. I'm declaring and decreeing that each individual that reads this is healed and transformed into new person so that they can receive what you have for them! I speak life! I'm claiming that my story will touch hearts and lives of the lost, the broken, the fatherless, the motherless, all that is less of what you designed us to have in life! I pray that you will begin to perform miracles in their lives as you did for me so that they will realize that there is nothing too hard for you! Give them the desire to be hungry for you, and as this takes place, Lord, I ask that you fill them up! Water those dry places in their lives so that they can grow in you! I'm claiming that they will walk away from this testimony with their heads held high, moving forward knowing that their help comes from you! Lord,

I'm thanking you for the willingness in their hearts to change. I thank you for what you have done for them already thus far by just wanting to seek more of you! We thank you for your healing, we thank you for your touch, and we thank you for our new walk in you! In the mighty name of Jesus, I pray, AMEN!

Notes

Notes

Notes

ABOUT THE AUTHOR

Jereme Wesley is a dedicated mother to four wonderful children. While currently fulfilling her dreams of saving the lives of others in her career, she has a newfound way of reaching out to individuals through writing, with hopes of making an impact.

Made in United States
Orlando, FL
10 June 2024